THE ROADMAP TO BUILDING A

MILLION-DOLLAR BUSINESS

BY

STEVE "RUFFCUTT" RAWLINS

ACKNOWLEDGMENTS

There are many people that I have met throughout my personal and professional life and each person I met has in one way or another led me to my successes and my successful failures. However, a few stand-out and I'd be remiss if I hadn't acknowledged them for their contributions. To Gerald (Jerry) Rhode whom I affectionately call "Pops," I'll never forget, thank you for your friendship.

To Matt Manero who introduced me to Grant Cardone' 10X crowd, and to Brad Lea; I observed, I learned, I applied and here is just one 10X goal achieved out of many yet to come.

My mom, the hardest working woman I know and has the heart of a thoroughbred.

Dennis Inman, you gave the greatest gift one could ever give. The gift of music I'm forever indebted, thank you.

So many have been an inspiration to me, and I thank all of you for your kind words of encouragement, love and support.

Ordering Information:
Quantity sales. Special discounts are available on quantity
purchases by corporations, associations, and others.
Orders by U.S. trade bookstores and wholesalers. Please
contact Steve Rawlins via www.StevenJRawlins.com/

Edited and Marketed By
DreamStarters University
www.DreamStartersUniversity.com

Table of Contents

"Associate with men of good quality if you esteem your own reputation; for it is better to be alone than in bad company."

George Washington

Chapter 1

Protect Your Blindside with a Budget

In 2008, my business was scaling on a level unheard of when the bottom fell out of the economy. Without warning, I was blindsided as were so many other business owners and entrepreneurs, and even though I had different secure revenue streams coming in with a client base that consisted of The Department of Defense, personal clients like CORPAC

Steel, the Jet Propulsion Laboratory, AutoZone and Blue Origin (which is Jeff Bezos' - Amazon's - rocket program) to name a few. I really thought I was secure. I tried to prepare for "the unknown."

Because I am good at making money, and spending it, I know how to use it and had several years of savings that I could fall back on if needed to get me through the troubled times. Little did I know I was staring into the abyss.

I thought I had plenty going. I owned a few different companies: a landscape company, an equipment sales and leasing company, a specialized heavy haul freight brokerage company and a heavy haul trucking company. Additionally, I was also consulting other people and helping them start their own businesses for a fee or part ownership. So, when things went south, I thought I was safe.

But by the time 2011 rolled around, things had gotten bad. That's when I had to fess up to my friends, family, business associates and clients that I was broke and had just enough money to cover my business expenses. I wasn't sure how I was going to pay my mortgage, let alone the electric bill.

Imagine having everything you could want within reason, and then being reduced to having only whatever would fit into the back of a '98 Chevy Blazer. That's what happened to me. I had become careless. I had become loose. Even though I knew the right things to do---to balance my budget and keep track of my finances and in the end like most people, I wasn't doing these things properly.

Many people I met while working as a business analyst faced similar situations. They had become burnt out, lost souls, who no matter what they had done or tried to do to salvage themselves and their businesses, they couldn't recover. So, they would turn a blind eye to their finances, thinking things would work out because they didn't want to face the realities of being broke.

Many people believe if they had more money it would solve their financial problems, but this is not true. People who make $100,000 a year or more report living paycheck to paycheck. 63% of the American population can't handle an emergency expense of $500.00 or more. A Gallup poll found only about 1/3 of Americans (32%) maintain a household budget. 19% have $0 saved to cover an emergency expense. 31% have less than $500 in emergency savings. 75% live paycheck to paycheck at least some of the time; 25% do it all the time

What's worse, many people have low wage jobs. The median income in 2015 was about $69,000 with $56,000 in expenditures, leaving only $13,000 in disposable income. To put that into perspective, that's a savings of only 4.31% of their income.[1] A lot of these people are good people working

---

[1] Financial statistics on this page pulled from: https://www.debt.com/edu/personal-finance-statistics/

their asses off, and they're not paid much. They're always broke.

Most I've found are just uneducated about finance, and they don't know how to create a budget. But for those who do have a budget, many fail to be disciplined enough to follow it. These are the people who fail to use their money in a way that benefits them, because they don't plan how they're going to use it each month.

They don't put money in an emergency account. They don't save anything for retirement. They don't save money for a big purchase down the line. They charge everything on a credit card, and because they failed to read the terms of agreement when they got that credit card, they don't take time to understand APRs, compound interest, late fees, and percentage rates of 29.99%. The next thing they know they are screening their calls from collectors, paying minimum payments, and floating checks. People just don't do the right things with their money, and this costs them big time.

Some of the signs you are living this way is you fail to stay on top of your budget. You have increased loads of debt. You start getting late notices on your credit cards, and you start getting collection calls. But many people take a head-in-the-sand approach to dealing with this kind of stuff, and they refuse to look at it.

When they do this, the cycle of debt begins to consume them. This is what started to happen to me, even when my business was doing well. The cycle of debt traps many people because they try to keep track of their money in their head. They don't sit down and draft out a budget on paper. They wing it, and they hope everything is going to work out okay.

But the truth is, if you can't manage $100,000 today, you're not going to be able to manage millions tomorrow. It's that simple. I always tell people to implement a budget. But do you know how many people do this? Very few do. As the statistical facts mentioned earlier prove, not managing your money well will lead to disaster if you're constantly shifting money around to pay the bills.

You might sign an agreement with a bank and say, "Okay, I'll take this amount of money from the bank, put it in my account, and I'm going to be responsible with it. I'm not going to charge anything to this account I can't afford."

But, then, some money goes out this way, and some money goes out that way. And before you know it, your balance has sunk below zero. Even if you make a small purchase, like, say, coffee at Starbucks, if you overdraw your account with that one small purchase, the bank is going to hit you with a $35 fee. Do this multiple times without knowing it, and that money you're paying in fees is going to start adding up.

The bank has no responsibility to stop you from doing this kind of thing. In fact, they thrive on this sort of behavior. They just keep charging you. They don't even notify you it is happening. Let me repeat that: the bank has no obligation to hold your hand and take care of your money. Your money is your responsibility. You must be accountable for it.

Unfortunately, people don't believe they have to be accountable for their money. Many people seem to think bankruptcy is a way out of things. They think, "Well, you know, I'll just claim bankruptcy if things don't work out." This is selfish, and it's also ignorant. It shows how much a person does not know about money.

During the recent subprime mortgage crisis in the United States, we all saw the fallout of what happens when people know nothing about personal finance. So, I'll explain something quick. When you get a loan from the bank, that money is not your money. The line of credit you get comes from the bank and is actually everyone else's money; it's the money the bank has been entrusted to loan out that belongs to everyone.

But people have the mentality that this money is theirs. If you have a mortgage, which most people do, you don't own your home. You are participating in a rent to own program. This is a big responsibility you've taken on, but people don't see things this way.

First, they get a mortgage, and then they start buying things for the home they don't own with even more money they don't have. They go to Lowes, and they buy brand new appliances with a Lowes credit card, when there's nothing wrong with the appliances already in the house. This is the kind of action and thinking that ends up causing big problems down the road.

If you don't believe me, just look at all the "fixer upper" type homes available out there on the market. These homes are gutted, run down, shells of the things they were meant to be because the people who mortgaged them couldn't afford to take care of them. It's not hard to find these kinds of real, tangible examples of people not knowing anything about how money works.

I've always been successful, and my business success would not have happened for me today if I hadn't learned how money works and how to operate a budget. When I started my first company, it was with a $15,000 investment I had saved up, and from that I built a portfolio of companies that had a presence in five cities, five states and generated over $23.5 million in a period of four years. I never would have been able to achieve this level of success if I had not known how to properly budget, invest wisely and have good spending habits,

I developed 401ks for my employees and for myself. Everything was set up as solid as it could be. This is what kept me going for years through the economic downturn I talked about already. To show you the difference this made, in contrast, at that time, about 500 trucking companies a week were going out of business during the economic downturn. Mine weathered the storm for several years.

I had to learn a lot of new things quickly when I first recognized the opportunity for me to start my own business. I started educating myself in finance, and I learned QuickBooks. I knew I needed to learn to do things I'd never done before if I was going to be successful. Once I'd learned these things, I started to appreciate them. They began to change my personal life, too.

When things went south, I realized I couldn't go out to the bar every other night or pay for everyone's expenses for an outing. Even though I was making good money, I couldn't just say to myself, "Let's take a week off, go fly around, and get hammered ass drunk." Nope. I couldn't do that sort of thing.

I've had bar bills as high as $2,800 in one night. But the party lifestyle gets expensive, and I recognized that right away. I realized just because I was making a good amount of money, it didn't mean I could get careless with it. I had to learn how to manage my money.

The best way to do that is by creating a budget. If you're a business owner, and you don't have one, you need to create one. Most likely, you already know how to do this. So, do it right now!

Ruffcutt Lesson:
Create A Budget and Stick to It

The path to true wealth is to save first, then spend what's left. It really is that simple, and the sooner you do this, the better off you'll be in the long run. You must learn to manage your finances. Create a budget you can stick to, and discipline yourself to manage and monitor it. This is essential. For if you can't handle $100,000 today, you will not be able to manage millions tomorrow. Though many people believe just having more money will solve all their financial problems, I've shown this just isn't true. It doesn't matter how much money you take home or how little, you'll never have enough. When you have money, hundreds are spent like twenties, and thousands are spent like hundreds. If you don't tell your money what to do, it will end up in somebody else's hands who will. It's as simple as that.

"I'll not go to the grave in a perfectly well-preserved body, rather I'm gonna round third base sliding into home plate all busted up, beaten and bruised shouting out, "That was one helluva ride"

-Steve Rawlins

Chapter 2

Do Not Be Afraid to Grow

Most businesses start as sole proprietorships. This is because people who want to have a business in the beginning don't want to get into all the complications with regards to taxes, regulations and government restrictions. But these are the things companies must deal with every day in the world of business.

As a sole proprietor, you're not high on the government's radar unless you're cranking out hundreds of thousands of dollars from the bank every year. But, trust me, if you're doing big business as a sole proprietor, and you're avoiding paying your fair share to the government, they're going to find your ass, and make you pay. And you don't want this to happen.

When I began my business, I took the time to educate myself about what type of company I needed to have based on the kind of business I wanted to create. This is important. You can't just go out there and ask an accountant or somebody what kind of business to set up. They won't know what your vision is for your company. You might not even know your full vision at the time of your asking for help.

As a business analyst and consultant, I often ask people questions about their businesses. I ask them, "Why did you choose to set up your business as this type of entity?"

And they usually say, "My lawyer told me to do it this way," or, "My accountant told me to do it this way."

Then, I must tell them, "Well, after my review, I must tell you, you've set up the wrong entity. You shouldn't be a _____. You should be a _____." This happens all the time. People take what other people say as the gospel, and they don't do their due diligence in figuring out what kind of business entity they need to create.

Some people will even call someone up, and they will ask them to set up their business for them. They'll send thousands of dollars off to someone to set up an entity for them that they don't know anything about. They don't even know the tax advantages they've gained or lost. In the end, they can't or don't even utilize what they just paid thousands of dollars to create. And this all happens because they don't have a clear vision for their company, and they don't take time to think about how they want to grow their business, or even how they want to begin their business.

Let me give you an example. Let's say your work is fixing cars, and you're doing okay money-wise. Not great. Just average. You might say, "Well, I'm comfortable with where I'm at. I'm just a small-time car mechanic, and I'm happy where I'm at, right here." But this is shooting yourself in the foot. If you say stuff like this, you don't have vision. You're just getting by. You're settling for good enough.

Vision allows you to expand your mind and use your imagination. When you don't have a vision, you're not going to grow. You're not going to advance. You're not going to do any better than anybody else out there who is just flying by the seat of their pants. Eventually, without vision you're going to end up dead broke. You need to understand where you want to go, or you aren't going to end up in a place you're going to like. Let me put it this way. Would you drive 1500 miles from your home to spend time with friends or family without having your GPS or a roadmap with you? Of course not. At least I'd hope not. So, why would you gamble your future using your livelihood as collateral?

When I started Rawlins, Inc, I took the time to educate myself, and I strategically developed a blend of business entities that would best serve my financial needs and take full advantage of the IRS tax laws. I ended up choosing an S Corp. Other company entities Rawlins, Inc held were LLCs or operated as a sole proprietor. So, think about the needs you have right now, or the needs you're going to have down the line. Then try to set yourself up with a business entity you can grow into. If you're already in business, start to take notice of the things that are happening in your business as it progresses and grows.

For example, when I began my landscaping company, not long after beginning it as a sole proprietor, I got a call from AutoZone, and they wanted a bid to put in irrigation, landscaping and trees around one of their new stores. This was a big contract, so continuing as a sole proprietorship was out of the question. I had to incorporate at that point, or I would have gotten killed on the taxes for this one job alone.

There are many advantages to incorporating, but don't shoot yourself in the foot choosing the wrong entity. There are many benefits to owning and running a company people don't hear about or take advantage of. But if you're willing to do the legwork and set your company up correctly, you can be a smart business person who knows what options are available to you and how they can benefit you.

When first starting out in business, we are all limited in our minds as far as what we believe our abilities are. This is a societal thing. We only believe we can do what we see others around us doing. But a proper vision and business plan is limitless. To reach new heights, you've got to go out on a limb. You must get involved. You must dig through the dirt and the shit, and you must find out what you want and how you're going to get it. In short, what's your long game?

If you just sit around and do nothing, you're going to get nothing out of business. We are all limited by our own imaginations and insecurities. The real reason for my success is I have never been afraid to tackle a problem I've come up against. Any time I have been presented a problem, I have found a solution, and I've figured out a way to profit from providing that solution.

Of course, if you're just getting your feet wet in business, it is okay to start out as a sole proprietor. But, what's important is you constantly expand your vision. You need to be constantly setting yourself up for the next step, the next level, the next best version of yourself and your business. Growth and change is good. Do not be afraid of it. *"I am not the same person I was yesterday that I am today, nor do I plan on being the same person tomorrow that I am today"* - SJR

Ruffcutt Lesson:
Own Your Vision

Vision: *To see the future for what it can become, not for what it is.*

Without vision, you can't plan nor lay the groundwork for what is to come in your business. If you don't take the time to educate yourself about what it is going to take to get your business to the next level, you're never going to get there. Setting up your business properly is the key to long-term success. Choose the correct business entity from the start and allow yourself limitless room to grow. Own your vision, and you will be able to take advantage of opportunities others might not even know exist.

"There are no bad decisions in life,

only consequences."

-Steve Rawlins

Chapter 3

The Building Blocks of Success

Once I started my first business, I was already bringing in a revenue stream from the irons I had in the fire. But there were other areas of the trucking industry I wanted to get into. These were the first steps of a long set of goals I set out to accomplish: I started Rawlins, Inc, and then SJR Equipment

Rentals and Leasing's where I leased specialized heavy haul trailers. At first, I was managing three heavy haul trucks, then seven. The next thing I knew I was managing 13 heavy haul trucks that were scattered all over America for a company and charging them 12% of the net. But my vision was to own a portfolio of companies and scale my business to extreme heights.

When you own a trucking company you generate a lot of cash flow, but there is just one problem: it takes a lot of cash to start a trucking company. Even though I knew it would take a lot of cash to start a company of my own, it was what I wanted to do. I knew it would be worth the investment. I've always subscribed to the theory that the best odds of achieving success are placed on me, not on Social Security or other government sponsored plans. I had a plan of how to get to where I wanted to go. I could see it in my mind's eye. I could taste, feel, and smell...SUCCESS.

But, how was I ever going to get enough money to start a freight brokerage company? See, this is where a lot of people get stuck when they first start a business. They might have a grand vision for what they want to do, but they can't seem to break it down into the building blocks they are going to need to stack on top of each other to get to their end goal.

I'll continue with my story to give you an example of what I am talking about. I began by starting my leasing company. I had contracts in hand for the lease of four specialized heavy haul units, and I was managing trucks for others for a fee under the Rawlins, Inc name and I was making bank. Most would have been satisfied at this level and would have milked it for all it was worth, but it was the leasing company and managing truckers that allowed me to raise enough money to start my own heavy haul freight brokerage company called Transportation Management Group, LLC. From there, the expansion of my business just happened naturally.

With over 35 years' experience in specialty fields of the trucking industry like Hazardous Materials and Heavy Haul Rocky Mountain Doubles and Triples, I was and am an expert in the trucking business, and I branded myself as such. I knew what problems were prevalent in the industry, and I knew I could provide solutions to these problems. I envisioned what I thought the industry should be like, and I made it happen.

As my company began to grow, I asked myself, "What do these truckers need?" Well, they needed permits. They needed pilot cars. They needed logistical support, and more importantly they needed someone who they could trust not to fuck 'em and give them an above average rate for above average work. I knew what my clients expected from me, too. I projected an image of professionalism with an air of confident arrogance, and I branded myself this way, too.

My guys didn't pull up to haul your equipment in some rat trap, piece of shit truck looking like shit. My guys came in with pressed shirts, nice jeans and work boots. They had safety gear and were extremely knowledgeable in their field. They knew this was old school trucking at its finest, and you were expected to conduct yourself in a professional manner. It was either that, or you were kicked off the site, and you never hauled another load for me again. In most cases, by the time I got done putting a guy through the ringer for fucking up, they didn't want anything to do with me anyway because they lost the war before it even began.

My guys had trucks that took a week of full-time work just to polish all the chrome and stainless steel. They had enough "chicken lights" to pull amperage from ConEd. These were the trucks that when you saw them going down the road, regardless of your opinion of trucking, trucks or truck drivers, you would gawk and talk about them for a while.

I began to provide my truckers with everything they could possibly need and more by creating different departments in my company to handle everything that might come up. This helped me in multiple ways. The first way was I was able to keep things moving fast within my company because I didn't have to rely on other people to get drivers road ready. I was able to provide drivers with everything they needed in-house to keep my loads moving.

The second way this helped me is through the profit I made from selling and providing these services to truckers. You see, all I was really trying to do was expand my business and make it more efficient. But the plus side to all this was that my revenue streams continued to diversify naturally, even though everything I was doing was in the same industry.

I would not have been able to make this happen for myself if I hadn't had a vision for where I wanted to go with the company. Although these changes happened naturally, I had to be open to them. I had to be willing to take the steps necessary along the way to get to my end goal. I had to keep my eyes open for different opportunities to present themselves and to make opportunities when necessary, too.

You would be surprised how many people aren't willing to do this. They create for themselves a huge vision for their company, but they don't have the will and passion to continue stacking the building blocks up on their way from A to Z.

I'm not saying you must have everything planned out. But you do need to remain aware of what you're doing always. You can't just get lazy and think things are going to run themselves or expect others to run them for you. You can't just expect everything to unfold on its own. You must pay the price to keep things moving. You must sweat blood to achieve success on a grand scale.

I have an extreme knowledge of trucking, particularly heavy haul trucking, and I exploited it. I knew what the problems were. I knew I could provide solutions. In the same way, you need to have an extreme knowledge of your area of business. This way you will be able to acknowledge when

27

there are problems, and then work to capitalize on them by providing a solution and expanding your business.

Sometimes the problems you need to solve to grow your business will be right in front of your face. In my case, I had taken way too many calls from truckers telling me, "You know what, I couldn't get my permit today. I'll have to get on the road tomorrow when I can get it."

My response, after I had created a department especially for permits within my company, was, "I'll call you back in ten minutes, we now have a permit department and we can make one for you. What's your fax number, brother?"

This is the kind of initiative it takes to grow a business. Not only did I solve a costly internal problem; I also solved an even more costly external problem, the loss of a client due to a delayed delivery. You need to know your industry better than anybody else, and you need to be ready to create solutions for your industry. There is no other way to grow a business that makes any sense.

The truth is, people sometimes start a business, and then they lose all their passion for the industry they are in. You can tell when this happens because then their business doesn't do well. They stop paying attention. They put their heads in the sand. They don't want to hear the bad news that they're in the red now. Then, eventually, they go out of business.

This happens because people get comfortable with where they are at. They let things get stagnant. They don't want to solve any new problems, just old ones. They don't grow or challenge themselves. It's your competitors that choose to solve new problems that are the ones gaining market share, stealing your customers and experiencing explosive growth. To make sure you're stacking the building blocks to get to where you want to go, you must keep your eyes open, and keep them squarely on the road of your industry. When you do this, there is no problem you can't solve.

When you're the expert in your industry, you don't have to wait for somebody else to solve the problem. You take the initiative. You make it happen. It's your duty as a business person to do this. And when you do it, you will have success. There is no other way.

Small business is how the economy grows, and how jobs are created, and this is just one way I contributed back to my country. This is how I was able to provide better jobs for people. I paid them better, and I treated them better. I allowed them the room to grow, and I would nurture talents they didn't realize they had. I invested in human capital.

I could see in people what they couldn't see in themselves. It didn't take long for my trucking company to accelerate in revenue to a degree in which I could finance more employees, health care, phones, internet, computers, everything you need to run a business and employ people. Hell, I'd even let employees set their own pay, and in every instance, they would lowball themselves when I asked, "What kind of salary are you looking for?"

While they were answering this question, I'd make calculations and ask them questions like, "Does that leave you enough to save? Will you be able to take a vacation and not ask if you can work through it just to have the pay because you can't actually afford a vacation?" There is nothing more satisfying to me than seeing the face on a person I just counter offered a salary package to that is over and beyond what they dared to ask for. You can see the relief in their eyes and the burdens of financial worries lifted off their shoulders.

But the ability to do this stuff wasn't all available to me in the beginning. I didn't just inherit some huge amount of money that let me buy whatever and hire whoever. If I had, things wouldn't have gone well for me. I'd have been too green and too dumb to run a successful business the right way.

But when you follow the steps, when you stack the building blocks to reach to the height of your goals, your success is not a question of if, but when. It becomes only a matter of time. So, enjoy the ride on your way to the top, and take people with you, too.

Ruffcutt Lesson:
Enjoy the Journey

You've heard the saying, "Life is about the journey, not the destination." This is easy to forget. But the journey really is the most important. To make sure your journey is successful, think of the moves you make and actions you take as building blocks you are stacking on top of each other. Each one leads you to the next great adventure in your business and life. You can't have a successful story if you're unwilling to experience the ride.

*"**Freedom** is never more than one generation away from extinction. We didn't pass it to our children in the bloodstream. It must be **fought for**, **protected**, and handed on for them to do the same, or one day we will spend our sunset years telling our children and our children's children what it was once like in the **United States** where men were **free**."*

Ronald Reagan

Chapter 4

Fat and Lazy

When I say, "fat and lazy," I don't mean that in a derogatory way. It's just the best way I can describe what I witnessed. When I was working as a senior business analyst, going around and analyzing people's businesses, my job was to find the root source of their problem. I was the one who had to go in there, find the root of the problem the business was having, and then report on it. I had to bring it out. I had to be the one to say the stuff everyone else wanted to ignore.

This is a tough job because not everyone wants to hear what you have to say. Some things just aren't popular, even if they need to be said. You can see this is true by looking at Donald Trump. Not everybody likes him because he says what's on his mind. He tells it like it is, and he isn't afraid of whether it's popular with other people.

When you can point out the root of a problem, and you're not afraid to bring it out into the open, it's the discussion that happens when you do this that brings change. It's called critical thinking, and I highly recommend reading *Winning* by Jack and Suzy Welch for more on this subject, particularly the chapter pertaining to candor.

If you're going to have your head in the sand and say, "Shut up, I don't want to hear this," then nothing is going to change. If you don't talk about what's going on, everything will stay the same. And if your business is struggling, this means you're going to continue to struggle until you eventually go out of business.

If you don't talk about the root of a problem, you don't promote critical thinking. Critical thinking is an important part of the recipe to success. You must do your due diligence to solve problems. If you don't provide an opportunity for debate, then that's close-minded. When I was working as a business analyst, this is where I learned the importance of telling people what you really think.

I had to go into different businesses, find the root problem, expose it, highlight it, and then bring it out into the open. After that, I had to convince people to act on what I had told them. I had to bring about change because of what I'd found.

This is tough to do because people don't want to hear this kind of thing. When they hire an analyst, sometimes what they want is someone to tell them everything is not their fault. They want the analyst blame somebody else other than them. They don't want to take responsibility.

I would go into tons of different businesses, and I would have to highlight things for them. I would have to tell them things like, "Well, you just told me your wife is an alcoholic, your kid who is supposed to be running things doesn't give a shit about the business and is running it like a piggy bank for his own personal use, and you, you're so damned burnt out, you couldn't give two shits about it, either. So, why do you think things aren't going well for you? Why should I help you? Matter of fact, I'm not so sure I can help you. I don't think you're willing to help yourself. Why am I even here?" Stuff like this was just a little psych game I'd play, and then the next thing I know they are begging me to stay and help them.

The truth is, when people get into these kinds of situations with their business, a lot of the time they already know what the problem is. I almost want to say when I give them my analysis, "You knew it all along. You just needed somebody like me to come in and tell you to your face what's going on."

Unfortunately, this was the case with most of the businesses I would go talk to. They didn't want to face their problems until someone shoved them in their face, and that's what I had to do, otherwise no change was going to happen. Their finances would be in shambles because no one was looking after them.

You know, a lot of people start businesses, and initially they're hungry. They work hard to get their business to a certain point, but then their vision dies, or it stops expanding, or they just get lazy. They get complacent, and over time they stop caring altogether. They get to the point where they don't give a shit about anything. The mess is too big to clean up, so they don't want to clean it up. They just want to keep getting by, every single day.

This happens with people's personal finances, too. Because, really, they are all connected. If you manage money poorly in your personal life, you're not going to manage it well in your business, either. In the beginning, a lot of people are willing to sacrifice to get their business started. But they lose that fire.

I had to raise $15,000 to start my company. To do that, I was eating $1.00 hotdogs from truck stops and drinking water out of my truck. I wasn't spending extra money. I wasn't buying sodas with all my meals. When I was raising that money, I couldn't afford to waste a dollar on anything that wasn't my dream. I wanted that company so bad I had to give up stupid, small comforts because I had irons in the fire like equipment contracts to finance, office space to lease, and fees to pay. I had such a narrow window I was working with.

I made all the sacrifices I could possibly make. I wanted that $15,000 more than anything, and I wanted it, like, right now. I wasn't partying. I wasn't spending money on parts trying to make my truck go faster or look better or anything like that.

A lot of people are like this in the beginning. They will do anything to achieve success. But once they've achieved it, then things start to go south. They start getting "fat." They start going out partying. They start having people over to party. They start paying for all kinds of things, and they lose their focus. When this happens, things start falling out of place.

Finances start going to hell, and they don't seem to care. When things get bad enough, it starts to affect their lives significantly in all areas. They aren't happy. Nobody working for them is happy, and they start to rely on other people to keep things moving in their business. Drugs and alcohol creep into their lives, then marital affairs, and soon they don't have the passion to run things properly and the whole business fails. When this happens, the fact is they have no one to blame but themselves.

I've seen this happen with too many business owners. For example, I got a call from a guy out in L.A. who owned a flooring company, and he wanted me to come out and do an analysis on his business. It wasn't going well from what I had gathered on the phone.

My scheduled time to meet with the guy was 10 in the morning. I showed up at his business at nine, and the doors were locked. This was during the work week, and this was a pretty good-sized business to boot. And, here, he wasn't even open at 9am.

It didn't even take a conversation with the guy for me to know what the problem was. This guy wasn't hungry. He wasn't generating hardly any money. I guarantee you if he was hungry, he would have been open at 4am when his contractors needed access to supplies and materials. But he wasn't. He'd grown fat and lazy. When I started my business, I was putting in 80-90 hours a week. This is what it takes to generate enough thrust to launch your company to levels of success most only dream of.

He was soaking people for money---his brothers, sisters, cousins, aunts and uncles---just to keep the place open. He was generating more and more debt every day. I knew he was burnt out. He wasn't even there. Nobody was and worse yet, nobody was making calls. There was no networking going on, and no targeted marketing strategies being carried out. It was more important for this guy to be somewhere else, doing something else, than for him to be at his business. I felt bad for this guy because he was just another broken spirit brought on by the economic crisis, and I could empathize with nearly these people I met.

When you lose your focus, I guarantee you everything will go to hell. It doesn't matter how hard you worked for it in the beginning. You've got to remain hungry. Don't become fat and lazy, or you're going to get your ass kicked in business.

Ruffcutt Lesson:
Don't Lose Your Focus

Everyone starts out hungry. Many people lose their hunger along the way. When they do this, everything starts to slip. They start to become lazy. They start to let things get out of hand, and they expect others to handle things for them. They even become unhappy in the process, and they start to treat their business and life as a chore rather than a privilege. To be successful, don't lose your focus. Don't become "fat and lazy." Surround yourself with people who will keep you accountable, and remember to always stay accountable to yourself, first. Remain hungry!

"Reject ordinary, be legendary."

Brad Lea

not the realities of who we are as a person, what stage we are at in life. We develop champagne taste on a beer budget. This all happens because ego sugarcoats reality to make our life more palatable. So, many business owners refuse to acknowledge when something is wrong with their business, and they pretend like everything's fine when they're running into the red every single month, and they can't pay their bills.

They think, "If I don't see it, it isn't happening." But this couldn't be further from the truth. If you're not willing to look at the problems and address the issues in your business and your personal life, they're just going to grow into bigger problems that are going to destroy you later.

You might think, "Well, I'm a John Wayne bad ass, and I've got my boots and hat on, and ain't a damn thing going to touch me." Meanwhile, your business is failing, and your family hates you and nobody wants to do business with you because you never keep up your end of the deal. This kind of stuff seriously happens all the time.

Ego gets in the way. I've seen this time and time again. People are not willing to level with themselves. I've had people call me in to help them fix their business, and the first thing they tell me is, "I can fix this. I don't need help. I've gotten out of holes before. I can do it again."

In one instance, I was met with such hostility that I finally had enough and looked the guy in the eye, and I asked, "Why are you so pissed off?" He didn't know what to say, and he just got that deer in the headlights look. He had nothing to come back with.

But the problem is what they're really saying is they aren't willing to look at the whole situation and admit they've got a problem they don't know how to fix. If they knew how to fix the problem and were willing to do it without being pushed, they wouldn't be paying me $1500.00 a day to come help them. Still, people would call me, and they'd tell me they wanted help with their business, but almost no one liked what I had to report to them.

I assure you that even though I was contacted by them, most all of them would be defensive, especially when it came to look at their financials. Holy shit, the attitude I would get from some people. You'd have thought I just opened Pandora's box, and in most cases these people's financials were a fucking accounting nightmare. People don't want to feel stupid, and I quickly found out the reason people get defensive about their finances is because they don't know finance, or they are trying to hide something.

Usually it was skewed entries that made the books look good. But I can see right through those. Many times, they just weren't doing things like they should have been. Take, for example, a simple balance sheet - not one business owner I ever did an analysis on could pull one up and print it off for me. Once I assured them that I was a professional, and that there wasn't anything they were doing I hadn't seen before, they would just give me access to their computer to get whatever information I needed.

Some people resisted my findings as if I had been personally attacking them. Why? Because of ego. When I go into a business as an analyst, often I am tasked with telling the business owner what they already know but are refusing to see because of their ego.

A lot of times, people want other people to fix their problems for them. They might even be aware of what they need to do to fix their problems on their own, but they don't want to put forth the energy required to do anything. They just want someone to come in, tell them what's wrong, and then fix it. In many cases the conversation would turn into them asking me, "Would you buy me out?" I had one guy, for the sake of peace in his family, offer to sell me his business for $125,000, which was generating $1.5 million in revenue per year, yet posted losses of $36k.

The problem for these people is, even if you fix the problem for them, it's not going to last. When you walk away, these people are going to go straight back to their old habits. They're going to start doing all the same things that got them into the mess they were in again.

If you're a business owner, you've got to recognize this. Otherwise you're going to pay thousands to other people to get them to solve your problems, only to realize you're creating the same problems repeatedly with bad habits you're refusing to acknowledge.

As a business owner, you've got to level with yourself. You've got to say, "Hey, I need to make this change. This is my responsibility. This is my company. These are my finances. These are my employees. This is my livelihood, and I'm going to do something about this right now."

This is the attitude you need to have every single day if you want to be successful in business. You must be able to be honest with yourself first. You must take responsibility for everything in your business and your life. You can't push things off on other people. They're not responsible for your success. You are.

When I first started helping other people with their businesses, I would often get frustrated. A lot of times, people would balk at my suggestions, and they'd have a hard time implementing them on the first stroke. Eventually their businesses would do worse, and the solution I would provide them the second time would be more difficult than the simple one I'd provided them with earlier on.

This is when I learned the truth of the adage, "You can lead a horse to water, but you can't make it drink." In the same way, I can't make you do anything I suggest you do in this book. My job with this book is to bring you to the water.

All throughout this book, I'm going to be bringing you to the water. I'm going to be giving you a roadmap for all the things you need to do or avoid doing to build a multi-million-dollar business. But even though I'm bringing you to the water, I can't make you drink it. If you don't drink the water, that's not my monkey to carry. That's your burden on your shoulders. I brought you here. I led you here. I opened the gate. I've done my part right. The gate is wide open.

First and foremost, level with yourself. Be honest about what you don't know, both to yourself and to other people. People think business is about having a big head and knowing everything and cramming everything you possibly can into your skull. But this isn't true.

You're going to need help. You're going to need people around you to show you the way when you're lost. You're going to need a map to reference when you get stuck. Business is not about generating more power for your ego. Business is about providing solutions for other people's problems. Success comes from changing people's lives through your product or service

To be able to do this effectively, you've got to be aware of your own problems and weak spots. And then you've got to be able to admit to them. Without that ability, you're going nowhere fast. You're like a horse standing at the water trough dying of thirst but being unwilling to take a drink. This is foolishness.

Level with yourself now. Level with yourself often. Your success depends upon it.

Ruffcutt Lesson:

Be Honest With Yourself At All Times

The surest way to fail in life is to live with your head in the sand or in the clouds. If you can't look deep within yourself and admit your own issues to yourself, you're never going to be a success. Everyone has issues. Everyone has areas of weakness. If you refuse to acknowledge yours, you're only cheating yourself. Be honest with yourself. See yourself where you're truly at, no pretending. If you can do this, you will cultivate the self-awareness required to excel in your personal life and business. The hardest thing to do in life is to examine it and identify and acknowledge problem areas that drag you and your business down.

"If your actions inspire others to dream more, learn more, do more, and become more, you are a leader."

John Quincy Adams

Chapter 6

Sacrifice

The hardest thing you're going to have to do if you're starting a business, or if you just want to take your business to the next level, is sacrifice. You will have to sacrifice to get to where you want to go. You will have to give up the pleasures maybe you've always enjoyed, like partying and fancy meals and fancy clothes.

When you're building a business, it takes a lot of energy. It takes a lot of focus. You will have to make sacrifices, so you can have the money you need to build momentum and get things off the ground.

There's something I've got to tell you about me. For me, sacrifice is where I started out in life. Let me explain. I grew up in deep poverty, and I grew up in an abusive household. There was alcohol around. I suffered mental and physical abuse. I always tell people, "My Keds were from the Feds." That's just how I grew up.

I didn't grow up knowing what sacrifice meant as a concept because I lived the definition of sacrifice. It was just my daily reality. You've got to have something first to be able to sacrifice it, and we never had anything. It's not like we were sacrificing when we never went on vacation and never stayed in awesome hotels or took trips or ate really good food or anything like that.

A lot of people think all that stuff is totally normal and necessary. And they think when they must start giving that stuff up, then they are really sacrificing a lot. But that's not the way I grew up. Those things were luxuries. When you grow up with nothing, you're painfully aware of all the shit people take for granted. When you grow up with nothing, you laugh when people tell you they're really pushing it and really sacrificing a lot because they only took one vacation this year, and they only eat out a couple times a week now.

I'm not trying to make you feel bad for me. What I'm really saying with this is that sacrifice means a lot of different things to a lot of different people, and you're the one who needs to know your limits, what you're willing to give up, and what you're not willing to give up.

How do you determine this? Well, you've got to figure it out on your own. You've got to figure out what's important to you. Your goal might be to continue to provide a high-quality life for you and your family. Isn't that the American dream? To give our sons and daughters a better life than what we had? But only you can determine what makes life worth living for you.

For some people, that might mean having a family. If you're in business, and you've got a family, and they are a priority, you make them a priority with what you do. You don't sacrifice them. That's just stupidity.

But if you're a single man, and you want to get ahead, you might decide not to have a family. *I always tell people, especially my kids - there are no bad decisions in life, only consequences*. You've got to decide these things and get your priorities straight.

What are you willing to give up to succeed? What are you not willing to give up to succeed? If you write these things down, you will have a good idea of where you're headed in the future. You see, there's no point in sacrificing everything that's truly important to you to succeed. Not only is this bad business, this is just a piss-poor way to live life in general.

But, if you're honest with yourself, you can determine the things you need to stop doing that are getting in the way of your success. Sacrifice those things, the stuff that just isn't significant. When you do this, it probably won't even feel like you're giving anything up in the long run because you're still going after what you've determined you really want.

When you make sacrifices, make them in a way that promotes a positive outcome. Make them in a way that benefits you. Otherwise, you're just cutting your own arm off and making yourself suffer for no reason.

Ultimately, being a business owner is just about being able to make the tough decisions. Let's say you've got to fly to Dallas to meet with a client, but your daughter has a recital or something the same night you're supposed to fly out. You've got the option of flying out early, getting to Dallas, getting some rest and missing the recital, and you've got the option to take a later flight that will cause you to miss sleep. This is when things get tough. You've got to decide, and that decision will have a consequence.

Now, if you're tired, and you decide to fly out early because you want to be ready for that meeting in the morning, that's a sacrifice. And it's a tough choice, because what you want to do is go to that recital, but you know you'll be exhausted.

But if you fly out early, and you end up acing the meeting because you've got the energy from sleeping last night, and you end up gaining a 1.5-million-dollar client, perhaps your sacrifice was worth it. But here's the kicker: only you can determine this. Although everyone is infatuated with success in terms of money, following your own principles is the only true determinate of success. You might keep score differently, and that's a good thing. Never. Ever. Sacrifice your character or your integrity in the name of success. If you do, you only cheat yourself and those you love.

Don't fail to recognize that as a business owner, you're going to be in these types of positions a lot. It's not always going to be clear the choice you should make. People don't like making choices. People don't like consequences. But not choosing is also a choice, and it too has consequences.

There will be things you have to give up on your way to success, small things and big things. But how you think about them is what will determine where you end up in the long run.

Ruffcutt Lesson:

Sacrifice is Necessary, But Pain is Not

Your attitude towards sacrifice is the most important. The truth is, if you want to be successful in business, you're going to have to make sacrifices. You're going to have to give things up. You're going to have to live a little bit differently than everyone else around you. But you don't have to think of the sacrifices you make as things you *have* to do. You can think of them as things you *get* to do. This will make a hell of a difference in the long run.

"The greatest day in your life and mine is when we take total responsibility for our attitudes. That's the day we truly grow up."

John C. Maxwell

Chapter 7

Home Vs. Office

I tried to do the home office thing ONCE. While everyone talks about how they'd love to work from home, until they do it, they have no clue what it's really like. I found it was a huge challenge. I found I needed to be in an environment that promoted critical thinking, and I needed to be in an environment that energized me. Working from home didn't work out for me because there were too many distractions.

You've got all your stuff at home - your TV and books and games and whatever you like to do in your free time. When you're working from home, it's so easy to get distracted by all kinds of things. It's so easy to find yourself watching something on TV, and you might even say to yourself, "Oh, I'm only going to watch ten minutes more." Then ten minutes becomes a half hour, then an hour, then the whole day is wasted. Soon you're not showering, and you're not wearing clothes that make you feel good about yourself, and you're not even shaving. Remember that movie with Jim Carrey called *Fun with Dick and Jane*? Yeah, that's you!

Your wife calls and asks, "Hey, would you start the dishwasher?" So, you do that. Then you get distracted by something else in the kitchen, food or something needs cleaned up. What happens when you work from home is you lose focus, and you get pulled away from what you're supposed to be doing, which is working on your business. Very few people have the discipline to say no to all the temptations that arise when you try to work from home. I am a very disciplined individual but working from home is just not for me.

I knew working from home was just going to lead to me becoming fat and lazy. My first office was a small office space that was dark, dirty and dingy, but I saw in it what others couldn't see. I saw potential, and the price was right because no one could see what it could become. I rolled up my sleeves. I put on my handyman, painter, and decorator hats and went to work. When the people I leased this office space from saw what I turned it into, they said, "Well, maybe we should have charged you more." I was generating more money in a week in this small office than their entire company made in a month

It's not hard to find unused office space. In fact, if you're trying to run a successful business, I recommend you get an office sooner rather than later. If not, you're going to be battling distractions all the time. And that's going to drag you down if you do it for long enough. You're going to get burnt out, and some days your willpower isn't going to be strong enough to get the shit done you need to get done.

Here's my observation: when you get an office away from the casa, things get serious, and they get serious fast. You start grinding because you've got skin in the game and responsibilities. A lot of times, people start businesses out of their home, and they treat it like a hobby. They do a little bit of work here and there, and this works for them in the beginning. This is not a bad way to get started. There is nothing wrong with it. As a matter of fact, many successful businesses started out this way. Bill Gates, Michael Dell, and a host of others all started out by working in their homes and turned their passions into major success stories.

But if you want to get serious about your business, and you want to take it to the next level, get an office. Get all your shit, pack it up and take it somewhere else other than your home or garage. Your environment matters a lot more than you think.

There is no way I would have achieved the success I have if I had been showing up to work every day in slippers and jammies at 10am. I'm too driven to even think about the home office lifestyle. I'd outgrow it within a couple of months, and you can, too.

I'm not saying don't start your business in your house. If you don't have the cash to rent an office space, for the love of God, don't rent an office space. But if things are kicking along, and you need to keep yourself steady, get an office space.

Most importantly, know when to get the hell out of your house. If you work on your business from home, and then you start bringing in cash like crazy, get the hell out. If you don't, you're going to start slipping. You're going to get complacent. You're not going to grow unless you continue to expand.

When I wanted to expand my market, I first needed to find the right people to hire to help me expand. So, I met a guy in Dallas, Texas, which is where I wanted to expand my business into. He was the right guy for the job, but there was no way in hell I was going to let him work from home.

I told him on day one, "I want you to locate office space and give me the details. I want you to work from the office, not from the house." Then I set a deadline for him to get this done. He quickly found a space at the Wells Fargo building on the 15th floor that overlooked Texas Stadium.

Now, the room wasn't much. It was maybe 20' x 20' but it was an office at an affordable price. It was a space where he could get work done. Within two years, I had this guy generating a little over a million bucks in revenue. He would not have been able to do this if he had been showing up to work in his slippers and robe. He would have been too comfortable. He would not have been disciplined enough to overcome the comforts and rise to the level I needed him to be at.

Trust me, if I can fall to the laziness temptation of the home office, then I guarantee anyone reading this right now can, too. And if you fall to this temptation, there is no way in hell you're going to become successful. Now, I'm sure there are plenty of success stories about people who have been successful in a home office. It's not impossible. But it takes an extreme amount of discipline, and most people just don't have it.

If you're battling distractions in your home office, take everything you've got, and make an office. You will be better off because of it.

Ruffcutt Lesson:
Get An Office Space ASAP

Don't get drawn in by the allure of the home office. Working every day in your underwear is not as great as it might sound. In fact, it's a surefire way to make sure you don't ever get any work done. Owning your own business isn't about seeing how comfortable you can make your own life. It's about pushing the limits of what you think you're capable of. It's about starting work at 5am, even if no one is making you do it. The sooner you move to your designated office space, the sooner you will begin to take on the full responsibility of running your own business. When you have room to grow, you will fill it. I don't know what it is, but each time I got a bigger space, I filled it quickly. Make no mistake, it is a huge responsibility, but it is worth it.

"Life is a marathon, not a sprint. It's about taking a bigger-picture approach."

Ivanka Trump

Chapter 8

S.W.O.T. Analysis

S.W.O.T. analysis can be used not only in business, but also in your personal life. S.W.O.T. is an acronym that stands for strength, weaknesses, opportunities and threats. Here is how you perform a S.W.O.T. analysis for your business.

What are your strengths? What are your weaknesses? What are the opportunities you have available to you? What are the threats?

It was Plato who said, "*The unexamined life is not worth living.*" If you don't examine your life and your business using some type of S.W.O.T analysis, then you're never going to get the full picture of where you're at right now and where you're capable of heading in the future.

For example, if I was to analyze myself, I would put down for strengths that I am good at understanding and reading financials and generating accurate reports about where businesses stand.

But, in all honesty, I suck at math. I really do. It wasn't until a couple of years ago that I really learned how to do long division by hand. I hadn't had a reason to learn it because I'd always used a calculator, but still, this is a weakness. I didn't want to admit this weakness, but I knew I must be honest with myself about it before it became a problem.

This is something I taught my kids as they were growing up. I would always tell them, "Always run to a problem. Never run from a problem." This is because when you run *to* a problem, you deal with it on your own terms. When you run *away* from a problem, you're forced to deal with it on someone else's terms.

So, you have two choices. You can either deal with a problem and like it, or you can deal with a problem and not like it. Either way, you're going to deal with it. There is no escaping it. Burying your head in the sand is not going to solve anything. It's just going to postpone the inevitable.

By understanding your strengths, weaknesses, opportunities and threats, you put yourself able to act. You put yourself in a position where you can run towards problems, understand them, fix them and make yourself and the situation better. It doesn't have to be a business problem you're solving. It can also be a personal problem. And it could also be a problem you're having with another person, like a friend or a family member.

You can do a S.W.O.T analysis of a friend, family member or employee to better understand them and to get along better with them. You can ask, "What are their strengths? What are their weaknesses? What are the threats they face? What opportunities do they have, don't have?"

When you begin to examine your life and the lives of those around you, you begin to discover new things no one else has discovered. You might run into a problem doing your analysis that you know needs solved. This could give you a great new idea for how to expand your business, because we know that business is just about solving problems for people.

The truth is, the process of S.W.O.T analysis never ends in business. You must be analyzing things every day, and you must make decisions based on the observations you make. What happened yesterday may not happen tomorrow. Sometimes things come out of the blue, and you must be able to examine them, and then take the best course of action.

Most people analyze things every single day, regardless of whether they are conscious of doing it or not. I guarantee you're already doing analysis in your mind every day. If you're not, you're not living, and you aren't running a business. You might be able to get away with doing your analysis in your head for a while, but if you want to take your business up to the next level, you've got to get specific about what you're analyzing.

You can't just fly by the seat of your pants and expect to make great decisions. Business just doesn't work this way. You've got to write things down. Get specific about the area you're looking at and analyzing and unpack it the best you can. Set yourself up to make the best decision. Set yourself up to be able to run towards the problem you're trying to solve with all the information at hand.

The game of business is always to be reaching for the next rung on the ladder, always to be moving forward and growing. What got you to the level of success you're at right now is not what's going to get you to the next level of success you're aiming for.

Ruffcutt Lesson:
Know Where You Stand

S.W.O.T. analysis is very beneficial because it puts in concrete terms what might feel very abstract if you were to do it only in your head. Writing this stuff down, analyzing it, and then deciding about your next action will set you up for future success every time. You can't fix what you don't know is broke. And you can't capitalize on a strength you don't know you have. Do a S.W.O.T. analysis when faced with a decision, and you will set yourself up for the greatest chance of success.

"The key to rapid success as a preeminent business is to fall in love with your clients."

Jay Abraham

Chapter 9

Business Lines of Credit

By getting started with small lines of credit for your business, you will set yourself up with the ability to get a larger loan later. This is basic stuff, but a lot of people don't think about it when it comes to their business. They think they can just do whatever they want with their credit cards, and everything is going to be fine. But this isn't true. It is hard enough to get money from banks for business purposes when you do everything right.

But when you're careless, and you don't pay up on time, and you buy things you know you're never going to be able to pay off, you're just setting yourself up for failure. It's best to take things slow. Start building your credit in small ways as soon as you start your business. This will help you out a lot down the line.

Getting started with small lines of credit will allow you to prove to the creditor you have a good history of using credit in your business. Like we've talked about in an earlier chapter, you need to be able to see your vision of where you want to go, and then you need to take the steps necessary to get there. Securing and using credit in your business is no different. It's a step-by-step process, and if you try to skip steps along the way, you're not going to succeed.

You need to understand how to use credit and how to manage it, otherwise it can totally wreck your business. But if you do your due diligence, and you stay on top of things, credit can help you out in a major way. Imagine scoring a huge contract that's going to bring in hundreds of thousands of dollars, if not millions---but, to meet the demands of the contract, you're going to have to buy a lot of equipment, maybe even hire a full staff to help you get the job done.

Well, if you haven't been building your credit, you don't have a lot of options. If you can't get the money fast enough to ramp things up and take on this contract, you're screwed. Even if you don't think you're going to need a huge amount of credit for your business in the years to come down the road, it is always better to have the option to get it than to not, because these types of things happen all the time.

In business, big contracts come out of nowhere when you're not totally prepared to take them on. But to do these kinds of jobs, you've got to put a lot on the line. You've got to get your infrastructure set up to really get things cooking. Remember the landscaping company and AutoZone in chapter two? Fortunately, I had the cash on hand to finance an operation like that, and if necessary I could have used credit to assist with even larger deals if they presented themselves.

Without using credit in these instances, sometimes you're shit out of luck. So, I always tell people to start building their credit early. No matter what. Start building your credit right now if you haven't already and be smart about it.

There are all kinds of services out there that will offer credit to your business. Then, they will sell you services on top of that, like credit monitoring and the like. But if you're always paying someone else to do this stuff for you, you're never going to build up an understanding of it for yourself. What you don't know can hurt you.

It was George Washington who said, "The smallest leaks sink the greatest of ships." How does this apply to what we were just talking about? Well, if you're constantly leaking out money to people to do stuff for your business you have no concept of, then that money leakage is going to sink your business over time! You need to know what is going on to be able to run your business.

Yes, you can outsource things you don't like to do. But if you're just outsourcing stuff because you don't understand it, your ship is just waiting to be sunk. You won't know when things have gone off course if you don't understand the reports people are giving to you.

I'm not saying you've got to be an expert in everything. I'm certainly not an expert in everything, and I don't claim to be. But I do have a good grasp of everything, and I know where things should be at. So, when someone comes to me with a report, I know right away what action I should take.

Understanding business credit has saved me a lot of money, headache and grief. And starting small is the way to go. If you can't manage a small amount of credit now, I can assure you your community bank is not even going to look at you when you apply for a bigger loan down the line.

When you apply for credit for your business, the bank is also going to look at your personal credit. If your personal credit is not up to par, you can forget your loan. You're probably starting to notice a theme throughout this book. I can talk about business until I'm blue in the face. And you can know as much as anybody about business, and still not be successful at it. But if you can't get your personal life in order as well, you're just not going to make it very far.

We tend to think of our businesses and our personal lives as separate things. But they aren't. They're connected. Creditors want to know what kind of person you are, and they want to see your personal affairs are in order before they hand you $300 grand.

So, start small, build your credit now, and later I can guarantee you'll be glad you did. When opportunity comes knocking, you'll be able to open the door and say, "Let's do this!"

Ruffcutt Lesson:
Build Your Credit Now

Running a successful business is all about being proactive. By building up your credit now in small ways, you will have larger amounts of credit available to you in the future when you need them. You never know when you'll get the call with an offer of the contract of your dreams. But when you do, you will want to be able to meet it head on. By becoming faithful with small amounts of credit now, you will be able to secure large amounts later to fund the big projects down the road.

"Fear is an illusion, YOU are REAL"

Gordana Biernat

Chapter 10

Networking

The type of business you have will determine what type of networking you should do. But it's always a good idea to network with other business leaders in your community. The way to do this is to get involved in your local chambers of commerce, Toastmasters club, even the B.B.B. You never know what opportunities could open for you when you do this.

When you meet with others, and they get to know you, they will naturally think of other people they will want to introduce you to. Business is really all about relationships, and the more you can develop the relationships you have with people who are out there getting things done, the better you will do in business.

Being a part of different organizations, doing charity events and staying active in your community are incredibly important. I recently volunteered for a charity event hosted by a group called the Women of the South. They are an organization that is heavily involved in fundraising for schools. It's not like my volunteer job there was incredibly high-profile, but by working as a volunteer, I put myself able to meet the people behind the scenes of this event.

I met a lot of individuals who are very active in politics, specifically county and local government politics, and they even offered to help me get into state government and politics. I've met high profile lawyers, media consultants and highly successful business owners at events like this over the years.

When you can get access to upper level decision makers, even if they don't work in your industry, there is still always opportunity waiting to open to you. The people in these positions, in most cases, got into these positions because they themselves have built a big support network. Chances are, they know people in all types of different industries, whether it seems like they would or not.

I myself am a social butterfly. I can engage in conversation with just about anyone. If I can't engage in a conversation with you, it's probably because I'm just catching a bad vibe from you. If I catch a bad vibe or get a handshake from you like I just wrestled a wet noodle, I stay as far the fuck away from you as I can.

To me, though, people are people. I don't care if you're completely broke and work at some shitty retail store as a cashier, or if you're the CEO of a Fortune 500 company---to me, people are people. I can talk to anyone, and I treat every single person with the same respect. It doesn't matter to me who you are or where you come from, intellect and the ability to converse is what I look for.

With this openness, I've gotten myself into a lot of interesting social situations. Once, I was waiting for a flight, and I met the vice president of a major financial services company. We chatted for a while, and we got along so well he invited me to come have a steak dinner with him and a client he was meeting with.

I couldn't turn down the offer. I cancelled my flight, and I stayed for dinner. In between heading out from the airport lobby to the restaurant, I decided to take some time to myself, return some calls, have my secretary decide arrangements for me, and to smoke a cigarette. Not thinking anything of it, I headed in afterwards to dinner, and I sat down next to Mike.

Across from me sat his client Jay, a high-profile tax attorney out of New York City.

The first thing Jay says to me is, "You smell like a Goddamn cigarette." This was this guy's way of testing me. He was a crotchety old codger, and I let him see the real me. And no, I didn't apologize for it because this is who I am, and I use it to my advantage. There is a reason my nickname is Ruffcutt. I'm cut from a rough piece of cloth and make no bones about it. I can be very rough around the edges, and I have quite the sharp tongue.

I choose not to wear my emotions on my sleeves, and if you want to play with sharks but can't stand the sight of blood, especially when it's your own, perhaps being an entrepreneur isn't your cup of tea. I suggest you rethink your career choice because you will get eaten alive. Sharks can smell blood a mile away, and your weaknesses are the blood that attracts the sharks.

Anyway, I wondered how far this guy would push me, but I didn't give in. I didn't start kissing ass just because he'd challenged me. I was kind of shocked, but not thrown off my balance. I'd met these types of guys before, a straight-shooter, real, no bull-shit talking type of guy. Without missing a beat, I fired back, "We all have our role in life to play, Jay."

He looked me in the eye with a turned-up grin and said, "What are you drinking?"

After the Vegas loads things were just getting going between us, the company sent out a guy named Lee to buy some equipment to send overseas to different clients. So, I set up a meeting with this guy while he was in the states. I flew out to an auction in Orlando to meet with him for the first time. I wasn't quite sure what to expect because when we spoke on the phone, he acted like a dick. But nothing could have been further from the truth. Things were already going great, so I knew we'd be working together a lot. But I like to meet the people I'm working with. I like to know them personally.

Generally, I find that people like to get to know me, too. I have a very large presence about me, and I believe this is because I'm a horse of a different color, and that makes me a unique type of business person. I have a little bit of a rebellious attitude, and I think people enjoy it. There's just no box you can put me in, and you can't stereotype me. I don't march to the beat of the same drum everybody else does, so I think this sets me apart from the rest of the herd.

Anyway, I went out to dinner with this guy, Lee, they'd sent to purchase some equipment, and we ended up meeting at this very touristy spot in Orlando, the kind of place where there are all kinds of stuff going on all the time, lots of little shops and restaurants and things to do. About halfway through the meeting, I knew things were going well. I knew we were clicking. I knew our relationship was developing nicely, and that we were going to make a lot of money together. I excused myself to the restroom, and as I was heading into the restroom, I noticed a little vendor stand where a guy was spray painting t-shirts with designs of whatever you asked him for.

On my way back to the table, I stopped at this stand, and I had a shirt made. I had the guy put two flags on the back of it: The United States flag and the Great Britain flag. Then I had him put both of our company names on it, mine and Lee's.

I walked into the dining area, and I sat down. I handed Lee the shirt and said, "Lee, this is for you." He looked at that thing, and he cried tears of joy. No joke.

The relationship was cemented from that day forward. After that night, things started to really ramp up for us. We both made a lot of money together in this business relationship, and we had a hell of a time doing it. All because I was the one who stepped up to the plate in a crisis moment and got the job done when it needed to be done.

If you're in business, be the person who steps up to the plate. Be the one who gets it done. This is what will get you the great clients who are willing to pay you what you're worth without compromise. If you kick ass for them, they'll kick ass for you. Make it happen.

I repeat---be the one who gets it done.

Ruffcutt Lesson:

Actions Speak Louder Than Words

Successful business owners come through when it's crunch time. They know actions speak louder than words. They get the job done with speed, efficiency and quality. If you make it a habit of acting for others when they are in need, you're going to find your services in high demand. Hone your critical thinking skills, and you'll go far.

"In the midst of chaos, there is also opportunity"

Sun Tzu

Chapter 12

Troubled Waters

Not everything is going to go perfect in your life or in your business. When you start to do well in business, you become much more susceptible to storms because of who you are and because of your position. I learned this from firsthand experience being successful.

If I was just a regular Joe, some things in life would not have affected me the way they did. Some things just don't happen to regular Joes, like winning at the lottery or jackpots on the one-armed bandit in Primm, NV, great things happen to people who are out there making things happen, who are going after their dreams and finding success on their own terms and making money.

The reason you become more susceptible to different troubles is because when you have money and success, everyone wants what you have, your home, the cars, the jewelry, your life. Everyone wants to be your friend. But these people, the ones that just want to be your friend when you become successful---they aren't true friends. They're only your friend because you have money. There are very few people who will stick around during troubled times.

But it's how you carry yourself through those troubled times, those troubled waters in your life, that predicts your ultimate success. When the storm's coming, can you raise your head above the clouds? Can you get a clear picture of what's going on, and can you decide about what you need to do about your situation?

When the storm is coming on, and the waters are clearly troubled, can you think with a clear head? This is very difficult to do because when you're in a crisis, you get caught up in everything that's going on. You become so enamored by everything that's hammering you from all sides. When your attention is being caught up in all these different problems, you forget to focus on creating solutions for them.

If you're not careful, things will start to slip. Even your mental health can start to take a nosedive, and then you might find those people who you thought were your friends don't give a shit about you. This might sound cliché, but this is all real. I'm being nothing but real about this stuff, because there is just no other way to say it. And this doesn't just apply to business. This applies to personal life, too.

There can be problems in your personal life that majorly affect how well your business is going to do, and there can be problems in your business that will majorly affect how smoothly things are going to go in your personal life.

But the real shit storm happens when you're on the verge of failure in business, and maybe you've got a family member that's having some issue you want to help them with. But, no matter what you do, you can't seem to help them. Remember, you can lead a horse to water, but you can't make them drink. Sometimes you might feel like you're just pissing in the wind. At the same time, while you're trying to help them, things are heating up in business. You've got demands to meet, and maybe your staff isn't taking things as seriously as they should.

When stuff is going on like this in both your business and your personal life, this is when it gets tough to rise above it all. But when it comes to just business, I can guarantee you're going to run into problems you never thought you would run into.

For example, once I got a call from a new client, an older gentleman. They wanted a big piece of equipment delivered quickly, so we did the job and the equipment got there in the timeframe they wanted it in.

Then one day, out of the blue, a registered letter came from some attorney's office. After reading the contents, I realized they were accusing my company and my employees of collusion with the dealer of purposefully shipping the wrong equipment. But I wasn't going to let them get in my head. I had held up my end of the deal, and I knew it.

They wanted me to settle, or they were going to sue. But my settlement was this: zero dollars and zero cents. We had done nothing wrong. We had followed the contract to a T. We had delivered the equipment when we were supposed to.

But I had to rise above all of this, and not allow emotions to cloud my thinking. I had to hold my ground. You see, some people in business are just sharks. They want to get at you. They want a piece of you. You can do everything right, and they're still going to try to eat you alive. They want to prove their dominance. It's not a question of *if* but *when* you will run into these types of business people. They are out there. But you've got to know when to stand your ground.

You've got to do your due diligence. If I hadn't taken the time to invest in myself and learn to understand contracts and agreements, when I got that letter from them, I would've had to go hire somebody to explain all of it to me. I would have had to hire a lawyer, and it would have cost me an arm and a leg.

Instead, I handled things myself. I spent about an hour looking over their accusations, and I responded to them for the cost of a postage stamp. It saved me a lot of headache just to deal with the problem right then and there.

This situation for the average small business owner would have turned into a huge legal nightmare. But I stopped it before it began. I ran to the problem, not away from it. When you run to a problem, you deal with it on your own terms. When you run away from a problem, you deal with it on somebody else's terms.

I saw that I needed to handle this thing before it blew up into something bigger. I saw what I needed to do. I saw that these people were trying to take advantage of me and my company, but when it came to slander of my employees, and company brand and reputation that's when things got personal, and I knew I had to bite. Hard.

In the end the attorney sent out another round of letters to all the companies that had taken part in this fiasco giving everyone "one last chance to respond." The letter stated that two had agreed to settle, and one hadn't (me). I never even dignified this letter with a response. It was weak and dripped of desperation, I never heard back from them again.

When the water is troubled, and it's rising, and the storm is raging, that's when you've got to be able to see things as they are. You've got to know beyond a shadow of a doubt that you're doing things right, and that you can handle anything that comes at you. Because many, many things will come at you. And you can't rely on the people around you to take care of your problems for you. It doesn't matter how great of friends they are or claim to be, you've got to take responsibility.

When you're successful, it means you're playing a different game than everybody else. You're out there in the shark tank with the big sharks that want to eat you alive. Be the bigger shark. Not to go out there and tear people apart, but to hold your own. To show people you mean business, and to show people you're not backing down. No matter what.

Ruffcutt Lesson:
Keep A Clear Head

It's easy to be distracted by the noise that is designed to confuse you when things aren't going right. When the waters are troubled, most people focus on the storm instead of steadying the boat among the waves. But when you keep a clear head when things go wrong, you can turn bad situations into opportunities. Stay focused on solutions instead of problems, and you will create your highest outcome, even when things go wrong.

"Either write something worth reading or do something worth writing."

Ben Franklin

Chapter 13

You Are Your Brand

Branding is always a hot topic when it comes to business. This is where a lot of people get hung up when they're just starting a business. They know branding is important, but they struggle to know where to start with building a brand. But, branding is just a combination recipe of a few things: quality and reputation.

Donald Trump is a perfect example of effective branding. People go to his resorts because of their reputation. They know they're going to have a high-class experience as soon as they check in. Everything is going to be high quality--- nothing will be below par.

Your brand must be the same. Make no mistake about it: you are your brand. It's not just about your logo and your website and all that stuff. Your reputation is what will build your brand and make it what it is. You are what will set you apart from everybody else out there.

I have always reflected my company's brand. And all my logos and things like that had to reflect my company. There is a psychological aspect that goes with branding as well.

For example, if you look at the FedEx logo, you will notice at the bottom of the 'E' going into the 'X,' there is an arrow. This shows something. This shows movement. This shows that FedEx is a company that gets things done.

They do the job---they'll take your stuff from one place to another as fast as possible, and if you need that done, you're going to hire them. The arrow in their logo is there intentionally, and whether you've ever noticed it or not, it has probably affected your perception of their company.

I started my first company out of the back of a semi-truck in San Antonio. On my website, SBAsolutions.org, my logo is in the bottom right. This is the one I sketched while sitting in the back of my truck waiting for this hot little number I'd met there to pick me up to go out. I drafted this logo because it represents me.

If you look closely, you'll see the road forms an 'S', which represents my first name. And the road is going through the mountains of Colorado, which is where I'm from. (Going through the mountains of Colorado with a truck is not as easy as it sounds.) I used red because of its intensity. I wanted people to know my company worked with intensity and purpose.

Brands do this kind of thing all the time. Go look at some different ones. You'll see all different types of colors representing different things. Colors convey a certain mood psychologically. For example, in the medical field, they use a lot of pastels and soft colors to convey calm, safety and competency, the kinds of things you want to experience when you must go to the hospital, which no one ever wants to go to one, but sometimes you must.

If you look at fast food places, you'll see a lot of yellows, blues and reds that encourage people to come in for a quick, flavorful meal. Wendy's is a good example of this, but they also do some other things with their logo to send a message to people. They used to have a regular bowtie on their logo. I'm unsure as to when they changed it, I just happened to notice this change one day while watching television. I never see a Wendy's commercial without noticing this now: if you look inside where the bowtie was, you'll see written in ketchup it says, "Mom."

Why would they put this in there? Well, they want your trust. They want you to feel like when you go into a Wendy's, your mom is back there making your burger and fries just how you like them. These sorts of messages are so subtle, and it's up to the business how they want to present themselves, but all businesses know this kind of stuff and put it in their logos and marketing. This is called brand positioning.

So, how do you position your brand? Well, to start, you must do what you say you're going to do. You must maintain your character by maintaining your integrity and not compromising your beliefs to get ahead. We've all heard the saying, "If you don't stand for something, you'll fall for anything." So, you must stand for something, because once you've tarnished your reputation, it becomes very difficult to recover.

Statistics say that if one person has a bad experience, they tell ten people about it, and if one person has a good experience, they don't tell, anybody---or they might tell like one person. So, when you're creating a brand, always keep in mind your company's values. Remember your mission statement. If you don't have a mission statement, you need to create one.

My very first mission statement was written about two weeks after I started my first company. This was it:

"We the owners of Transportation Management Group hereby pledge to make sound and careful decisions thereby allowing our employees, customers, carriers and community to benefit from those decision. We pledge to promote our employees' success by providing the tools necessary for ongoing growth and education in the industry. We actively participate in the community and the transportation industry, which reflects our commitment to community by having a positive influence on others."

You'll notice I mentioned my employees several times in this mission statement. The reason I did this is because I wanted them to share the same vision I had for the company. When you can share your vision with your employees, they will be motivated all day long. You must be able to tell a story that they are a part of to motivate your employees.

See, your brand isn't just for people outside of your company. That's part of it. But your brand is also for people inside of your company. You need to pay leading wages. Why? Because if you don't, your best people are going to go work somewhere else. And your best people are what's going to make your brand standout in the marketplace. They are the ones who are going to get things done for you the right way the first time, and make you look like a Rockstar to all your clients.

Then, another part of your branding is investing in your clients. We can talk about pretty images all day and how to set up a website, but if you aren't building relationships with your clients, no looking logo is going to start printing your money. When you invest in other people, you invest in yourself. Whatever you put out there comes back to you ten times over.

When you are dedicated and loyal, you get dedication and loyalty ten times over. Your job as a business owner is to build your brand this way. Don't get caught up in having a fancy website or a fancy social media page. All you need to do is invest in people, and then monitor your business as it grows. Make sure you're keeping on track with your mission statement. Make sure you're building a name and a brand you can stand behind, something that reflects your core values.

Branding is more than just a logo. Branding is who you are. Who you are now affects who you are in the future. Remember all of this, and you are on your way to building a brand that is unforgettable. Once you've done that, then you can focus on the small things like having a nice logo and a nice website. But don't ever put those things first. That's putting the cart before the horse.

Your brand is you. Invest in yourself. Invest in your education. Invest in your employees, clients, products and services. This is the truth of how you build a strong brand. I'll say it again: branding is more than just a logo. Your branding is you. Carry yourself well, and your brand will grow strong.

Ruffcutt Lesson:
Build A Strong Reputation

These days, people think branding is all about being flashy and standing out. But this isn't true. Building a strong brand is about building a strong reputation in your industry for quality and dependability. A great logo isn't going to do anything for you if you can't deliver on the things you promise to your clients.

"Doubt is your enemy."

Grant Cardone

Chapter 14

Do Something, Even If It's Wrong

It's not a coincidence I've saved this chapter for last. I don't mean to blindside you with this statement, but it's the truth---you can forget everything I wrote in the previous chapters and still be successful in business. You will save yourself a lot of trouble if you heed the wisdom I've given to you in the preceding chapters, but you don't have to.

You can totally ignore it, and I can guarantee you you're going to learn some hard lessons if you do. But you can ignore it, learn the lessons the hard way on your own, and go on to be extremely successful. You really can. But, you can't take this chapter lightly. This is where the rubber meets the road. This is the meat and potatoes of everything.

Working in the oil and gas industry is tough work. If you wear your emotions on your sleeves in this industry, everyone will eat you alive. They will literally send you packing your shit and "run you off." They force you to man up.

I was once hired by a pipeline company to transport their heavy equipment, and being new to the company who hired me, I was kind of unsure of their expectations and what not. (Understand Maslow's Theory and you'll understand this) Anyway, one day out on the job site, I got a call from the boss out of the blue, and he said, "Hey, did you get that track hoe over to the site yet?"

And I said, "No, I haven't because I was waiting on you to tell me you needed it."

He, Jerry, said to me, "Goddamn it, son, do something, even if it's wrong." This lesson has stuck with me ever since. Do something, even if it's wrong. There are people out there who won't do anything unless they're told to do it. They won't pick up the phone and call that dream client because they haven't yet figured out exactly what to say. I call bullshit. Make that call. Say something. Even if you make a fool of yourself, it's better than sitting on your ass and waiting for something to happen. You're guaranteed to look a fool then.

Acting is how you get started. How do you start in the morning? Well, you start by getting out of bed. You take a shower. You make your bed. You get dressed. There are all these steps you take to get your day going, but people don't look at doing business this way.

People don't apply these same principles of getting started to start their own business. They get worried about what people might say. Even I still run into this problem. I ran into this problem when I sat down to write this book. I thought, "Well, I don't really have all the facts in front of me yet. I'm not sure 100% where I want to go with this thing." But, I quieted that part of my mind, and I got started.

As people, we get afraid when we want to do something new. Then, a lot of people don't even try something new at all because they're afraid of failure. They're afraid of what other people are going to think. They become afraid of what their friends and family are going to think. They don't want to get out of their comfort zone and upend the apple cart and all that.

But you must be different if you want to be successful. If you start, you're automatically different. And if you start something, your next step is to finish it. Don't be concerned about what somebody else might think.

You can't go around believing everything is way over your head and you'll never be able to handle it. Things might seem intimidating at first, but that's because you've just never handled them directly before. By seeing the problem, recognizing it, learning how to solve it, and then solving it, you are making huge strides, even if you fuck things up along the way.

You must do something, even if it is wrong. You must have faith that things are going to work out how they're supposed to. You must have faith in your business, your idea and the team you've put in place to run everything. Once things get moving for you, and momentum is really starting to build, you'll see other people come alongside you that will add to your confidence.

But in the beginning, trust me, no one is going to believe you. If you're gutsy enough to start a business, you're going to have to learn how to take the bumps and bruises that come with messing things up along the way. And no one is going to be there to patch you up. You must patch yourself up on your own. It's the only way you're going to get your skin thick enough to stay in business for long.

You've got to believe in yourself just like I had to when I started my first business out of the back of my truck. The first thing I did was set up the sleeper of my truck into a portable office complete with a coffee pot, a wifi card and a tv tray as a desk so I could get online with my computer in the back of my truck. I got a little personal printer, so I could print things when I needed to. I didn't have a lot of resources or money or anything. I basically started with nothing. I had to work my way all the way from the bottom to the top.

If you skip the story from the bottom to the top in your life, I guarantee you will not have success. If you skip the journey, you'll miss the success. Success won't even feel like success to you because you'll always be insecure, and you'll always want more.

Everybody thinks to start a business you need to already have money. But this couldn't be further from the truth. Everyone is always saying things like, "Well, if I only had a hundred thousand dollars, then I could have a successful business." But this is not the answer.

If you can't help yourself, no one will help you, and no one in their right mind should help you. In the long run, if you can't help yourself, you will just drain all your resources and other people's resources besides. When I first started out, I put 100 percent of myself into my company. I was there early. I was there late. I was working my ass off.

But as my company grew, I needed to grow. I needed to get better at time management. I needed better organization, because I couldn't keep working 24/7. That's not sustainable, and it's bad business. As your business grows, you must know what changes to make to make things run better for you.

You don't want to micromanage people. Nobody likes that, and it's not a good use of your time. As your business grows, you must have confidence in your employees, just like you had confidence and faith in yourself to grow the business up to that point.

Remember, though, it all starts with you. Have faith. Go out there and do something, even if it's wrong, and you will be amazed at what you can accomplish along the way. And don't skip the journey. When you look back on it all, the journey is the true reward. All the rest of it is just smoke and mirrors. Stay true to yourself, keep investing in yourself like you have done by reading this book, and keep your eyes on the road. You can do this. I know you can.

Ruffcutt Lesson:
Act Now, Think Later

People waste too much time thinking about doing something. You can always adjust later if you happen to take the wrong action now. But if you just sit there thinking about starting a business, you're really doing nothing. It is better to act now and think later. Do something! Then adjust your strategy based on what you've learned. This is the only way real way to learn. Have faith in yourself, your idea and your business! Act today, because you deserve success. It is your duty to seek out success. If not for you, do it for those you care about!

I barked back, "Scotch on the rocks." And the scotch flowed all night. I pretty much kept my distance from Jay for the rest of the night, and everything turned out great. I had a good time, and everybody else did, too. At the end of dinner, Jay handed me his personal card with his personal phone number on it, and he extended an open invitation to call or come out and visit him at his private ranch and golf course any time.

Although I accepted the dinner invitation that evening, I never made that phone call. When you're invited to the table, there's a certain level of respect you've got to display. I could have easily put Jay in his place that evening, but instead I played it cool. I didn't let my guard down, and the result was I had good favor with the VP of a major financial institution, and I was granted access to a level of money that is generally reserved for those that are "distinguished." This is when I learned money works for different people on different levels.

I never made the phone call to Jay because I just didn't like the guy's vibe. I could tell he was toxic, and I don't do business with toxic people just because they're powerful or can wield a lot of cash. But, still, I maintained the connection with this guy. I didn't burn the bridge just to burn it. If I wanted to call the guy tomorrow, I could. But I won't because I don't compromise my character or my integrity, and I'm not desperate. I came from nothing, and I'll leave this world with nothing.

Plenty of people would have taken him up on the offer to go out to his ranch and get favor out of him since they'd fallen under his good graces. In fact, most people would. But not me.

Let's assume I called him up, and I tried to work out deal with him. He would probably say, "Yeah, I'll make the deal, Steve, but inside you know, there are going to be terms, and they won't be yours." Accepting those terms would mean compromising my values, and it would mean I was now the pawn and not the king.

The way I do life and business is with the principle that just because someone has success and money doesn't give them any type of authority over me. I don't compromise myself in exchange for something trivial. I don't work with people who I know are toxic. I might have dinner with them. I might get to know them. But if I can tell someone is toxic right off the bat, it's a no go.

Never compromise who you are, because if you do, you're nothing more than a money whore, and someone will spot that and take everything from you. Why? Because they can. You can play with toxic people all you want. You can make them like you. But don't ever do a deal with somebody you know will screw you over the second they get a chance to. You're worth just as much as anybody who has already obtained success, even if you aren't successful. If you carry this attitude into all your networking, you're going to find

yourself in some amazing places, meeting amazing people very, very fast.

Ruffcutt Lesson:
Treat Everyone the Same

Everyone has a role to play in life. You never know when or where you're going to meet someone who is going to open brand-new worlds of opportunity for you. Always put your best foot forward. Get involved in your community. Make use of your connections but stay true to yourself. Trust your gut. Build your network, and watch good things happen for you.

"What separates the winners from the losers is how a person reacts to each new twist of fate."

Donald Trump

Chapter 11

Be the One Who Gets It Done

One day I got a call from a panicked client whose client was bringing in new road construction equipment by boat from Scotland. This was very heavy stuff, like road machinery equipment, pavers, and scrapers. The company was new, and they were headed for the Las Vegas Heavy Equipment Show, which is a trade show for the industry that happens only once every five years. It was a big deal for them to be there and showcase their heavy equipment.

The problem was, the boat that was supposed to be bringing in their equipment had suffered some problems on the way over to the United States, and it had even sprung a leak. Because of this, they had been forced to come in to land way off course, somewhere in South Carolina, a long way from the original port of entry which was supposed to be the port of Houston.

The client was in absolute distress. On the phone, he was like, "Oh my God. I don't know what we're going to do. We have to have these things there like tomorrow." They had a very, very small time-frame to get everything to Vegas for the show, and if they missed it, they were going to be eating some major costs with nothing to show for it

Just one piece of the equipment alone weighed like 120,000 pounds. It was a huge load. It required specialized hauling equipment, an expanded trailer and the right people who could get it moved safely and quickly. There were several pieces that needed moved, and the deadline was something ridiculous. Anyone not experienced with this stuff couldn't have done it. These were very technical moves and given the timeframe, not for the faint of heart

But I wasn't flustered at all by what needed done. My response to the frantic man on the phone was, "Yeah, we can do that." And my team of qualified people made it happen. As a matter of fact, the last piece of equipment got to its destination one hour prior to the cutoff time all the equipment

had to be there. I got the job done, and I did it with skill and expertise.

This was the start of a relationship between me and this company, who was based out of the UK. One of the major things this company decided they were going to start doing was buying equipment here in the United States, and then selling it and shipping it out to the UK and Germany and other places all over the world. They needed a contact in the states, and they needed someone they could trust, someone that could guide them. They needed access to someone who had access to highly specialized equipment to do this.

Guess who their first choice was to become their exclusive carrier. Me. Then they decided they wanted to open an office in Houston. I became a key player in helping them start this office, too.

I became the person they always called. They were always asking me for help. And when you're an expert like I am, that help doesn't come cheap. We did lots and lots of money together, and this was all because I had already proven to them what I was capable of. I was able to charge higher rates because I was simply the best at what I was doing for them, and they knew it, and they never balked.

Now, my success with this company wasn't solely because I was the best in business at hauling heavy loads. My success can also be attributed to my being able to build a relationship with them.

"Your content is like clay. You can shape it, adjust it, and perfect it."

Hank Norman

As you move along in your journey, there will always be people who do not want to make change. I will tell you from experience that the entrepreneurs who make it in this world know how to adapt to change. If you want to build a million-dollar business, you will have to welcome change with open arms. Then, figure out how to win. Otherwise, you will end up in a world of mediocrity. This cartoon says it all:

Be ready to change.

For more information on Steven J. Rawlins speaking events, seminars, coaching, and services, please visit:

www.StevenJRawlins.com

Facebook Profile: Ruffcutt Rawlins

Facebook Business: SBASolutions

Twitter: RuffcuttRawlins

Instagram: Steve_Ruffcutt_Rawlins

Linkedin: Steve Rawlins